69621
STAR OF THE JAZZ

and a short history of the N7 class of locomotive

EARM PUBLICATIONS

a division of East Anglian Railway Museum (Trading) Ltd.

EARM PUBLICATIONS

Chappel & Wakes Colne Station, Colchester, CO6 2DS. Tel. 01206 242524
a division of East Anglian Railway Museum (Trading) Ltd., the trading
subsidiary of East Anglian Railway Museum, a Registered Charity No. 1001579

Publishing History:
First published by EARM Publications 2021

ISBN 978 1 9168788 0 8
British Library Cataloguing In Publication Data.
A catalogue record for this book is available from the British Library
© East Anglian Railway Museum 2021
Typeset and designed by EARM Publications

Printed by Crescent Card Company, Tiptree, Colchester, Essex

INTRODUCTION AND ACKNOWLEDGEMENTS

This book has been compiled by a team from the East Anglian Railway Museum, and we would like to thank all the photographers whose work has been used, and they are individually credited. In addition, thanks must go to Pete Martin, Nick Proud, Mark Honeywood, Mark House, John D Mann, G D King, Michael Sanders, Andy T Wallis, Steve Allen and Geoff Hutton for all their assistance.

Front cover: N7 69621 in action at the East Anglian Railway Museum on 30 May 2011 (Kieran Hardy)

Inside front cover: N7 69621 at Liverpool Street station on 27 August 1960 (Colour-Rail)

A brief history of the N7 class locomotives

The story of the N7 locomotive goes back in some respects to 1903 when the City & North East Suburban Electric Railway put forward a Bill to Parliament for a new electric railway that would have taken much of the Great Eastern Railway (GER) suburban traffic. The GER produced a 0-10-0T (named the "Decapod") to demonstrate that steam traction could accelerate trains as fast as the proposed electric trains and saw off the challenge to the GER's suburban traffic. Whilst Decapod proved it could better the requirement to accelerate a load of 300 tons from rest to 30 mph in 30 seconds it was a specially built one-off. Decapod was rebuilt as a 0-8-0 tender locomotive in 1908 and was principally used to haul coal trains. The locomotive was withdrawn and scrapped in 1913. Had a class of Decapods been built their weight would have required a lot of permanent way and civil engineering upgrades. Apart from this one trial locomotive, the suburban services remained in the hands of 0-4-4Ts, 2-4-2Ts and 0-6-0Ts before the First World War.

The appointment of Alfred John Hill in 1912 as Locomotive Superintendent of the Great Eastern Railway proved to be the catalyst for a new design of locomotive, to be the GER's first 0-6-2Ts. Hill was a GER man throughout his life: having started with a six year apprenticeship in 1877 he worked his way up through the ranks until achieving the post of Locomotive Superintendent, a post he was to hold until his retirement in 1922. In early 1915 the first pair of new 0-6-2 tank locomotives entered traffic numbered 1000 and 1001. The GER used Stratford Works order numbers to identify locomotive classes so they became the L77 class. They were an inside cylinder piston valve design with Walschaerts valve gear, quite unusual at the time for an inside cylinder design. The front axle boxes and coupling rods were designed to allow the front axles to traverse sideways and so enable the locomotives to negotiate sharp curves more easily. In accordance with GER practice both locomotives were right hand drive and fitted with Westinghouse air brakes. There were significant differences between the two locomotives though. No.1000 used saturated steam and was painted in light grey, lined out in red with black edging, whilst No.1001 had a 12 element Robinson superheater and was finished in GER blue passenger livery. They had cast brass numberplates on the bunkers, but these were replaced by large yellow numbers painted onto the tanks in 1921. Number 1001 was the only 0-6-2T to carry GER blue passenger livery.

Both locos were fitted with condensing pipes. This meant that the exhaust steam could be condensed when working in tunnels so keeping the atmosphere clearer. Given that the first station out of Liverpool Street at that time was Bishopsgate, and the platforms on the west side were effectively subterranean, this was useful. (The site of this station is clearly visible to this day: one of the platforms was decorated with the flags of the participating countries in the 2012 Olympics). However the station closed on 2 May 1916 as part of the GER's war effort to reduce manpower requirements to release more men to participate in the Great War - and was never to re-open. The locomotives were of a compact nature, with the length over the buffers being 34 feet 10 inches – about the same as the 2-4-2Ts they were to supersede. As the new design was compact it meant that no expensive changes were required to run round loops etc. Weighing 61 tons 12 cwt, the driving wheels had a diameter of 4ft 10ins, the trailing wheels 3ft 9ins.

Due to the First World War and the immediate post-war backlog of essential repairs no more 0-6-2Ts were ordered until April 1920 when an order was placed for a further ten locomotives. These were the K85 class and were numbered 1002-1011. Even though the superheater fitted to 1001 had shown its worth post war material shortages meant these were not superheated, they were delivered during the period July to November 1921. They carried a new livery of lead grey with black lining, and the GER initials on the tank sides in yellow lettering with black shading. All of this batch were fitted with condensing equipment and were fitted with Westinghouse air brakes only. As well as the Enfield and Chingford services the initial two locomotives operated on, this new batch extended their sphere of influence with runs as far as Witham.

As originally numbered 999E, this is at an unknown location but probably at Stratford. It is possible that this photo was taken immediately prior to entering traffic, as the locomotive was renumbered to 7999, c1924
(Lens Of Sutton Association)

The July 1922 timetable showing the intensity of the evening peak departures from Liverpool Street on the lines to Palace Gates and Enfield Town

LONDON, PALACE GATES, and ENFIELD TOWN.—Great Eastern.

Down. Week Days—Continued.

	E	E	S	E		E	E	S	E		E	E				E	E	S	E		E	E	S	E		E
	aft	b	aft	aft	aft	aft	b	aft	aft	aft	aft				b	aft	aft	aft	aft	b	aft	aft	aft	aft	aft	b
Liverpool Street..dep.	5 10	5 14	5 20	5 20	5 24	5 30	5 34	5 40	5 40	5 44	5 50	....	5 54	6 06	06	46	106	146	206	206	246	306	34
Bethnal Green	....	5 18	....	5 24	5 28	....	5 38	....	5 44	5 48	....	5 58	....	6 46	8	6 18	....	6 246	28	....	6 38
Cambridge Heath	....	....	5 25	5 26	....	....	5 45	5 46	....	....	6 56	6	....	6 256	26	....
London Fields	5e17	....	....	5 29	....	5 37	....	....	5 49	....	5e57	....	6 9	....	6e17	....	6 29	....	6e37
Hackney Downs	5e19	....	5 29	5 31	....	5 39	....	5 49	5 51	....	5e59	....	6 96	11	....	6e19	....	6 296	31	....	6e39
Rectory Road	....	5 26	....	5 34	5 36	....	5 46	....	5 545	56	....	6 6	....	6 146	16	....	6 26	....	6 346	36	....	6 46
Stoke Newington	5 23	5 28	5 33	5 36	5 38	5 43	5 48	5 53	5 56	5 58	6 3	....	6 86	136	186	236	286	336	366	386	436	48
Stamford Hill	5 26	5 31	5 36	5 40	5 41	5 46	5 51	5 56	6 06	16	6	....	6 116	166	206	216	266	316	366	406	416	466	51
Seven Sisters	5 28	5 32	5 39	5 42	5 43	5 48	5 52	5 59	6 26	36	8	....	6 126	196	226	226	286	326	396	426	436	486	52
Seven Sisters ...dep.	5e32	5 33	....	5 45	5e52	5 53	....	....	6 66	812	....	6 13	....	6 25	....	6 336	396	446	456	52	6 53
West Green	5e35	5 36	....	5 48	5e55	5 56	....	....	6 86	815	....	6 16	....	6 28	....	6 366	42	6 476	48	6 55	6 56
Noel Park *	5e39	5 40	....	5 52	5e59	6 0	....	....	6 126	19	....	6 20	....	6 32	....	6 406	846	516	52	6 59	7 0
Palace Gates †	5e42	5 43	....	5 55	6 26	3	....	....	6 156	22	....	6 23	....	6 35	....	6 436	496	546	55	7 2	7 3
Bruce Grove	5 31	....	5 41	5 45	5 46	5 51	....	6 06	56	66	11	....	6 216	256	266	31	....	6 416	456	466	51
White Hart Lane	5 34	....	5 44	5 48	5 49	5 54	....	6 46	86	96	14	....	6 246	286	296	34	....	6 446	486	496	54
Silver Street ‡	....	....	5 47	5 51	5 52	5 57	....	6 76	116	126	17	....	6 276	316	326	37	....	6 476	516	526	57
Lower Edmonton 306	5 39	....	5 50	5 53	5 54	5 59	....	6 106	136	146	19	....	6 306	336	346	39	....	6 506	536	546	59
Bush Hill Park	5 43	....	5 54	5 57	5 58	6 3	....	6 146	176	186	23	....	6 346	376	386	43	....	6 546	576	587	3
Enfield Town ...arr.	5 46	....	5 57	6 0	6 1	6 6	....	6 176	226	216	26	....	6 376	406	416	46	....	6 577	07	17	6

Down. Week Days—Continued.

	E	S	E	E			b																				
Liverpool Street..dep.	6 40	6 406	446	506	547	07	107	207	30	....	7 40	7 50	8	08	158	308	459	09	159	309	4510	010	1510	30
Bethnal Green	....	6 446	48	....	6 587	4	....	7 24	....	....	7 44	....	8 4	....	8 34	....	9 4	....	9 34	9 49	10 4	....	10 34
Cambridge Heath	6 456	46	....	....	....	7 6	....	7 26	....	....	7 46	....	8 6	....	8 36	....	9 6	....	9 369	51	10 6	....	10 36
London Fields	....	6 49	....	6e57	....	7 9	....	7 29	....	....	7 49	....	8 9	....	8 39	....	9 9	....	9 399	54	10 9	....	10 39
Hackney Downs	6 496	51	....	6e59	....	7 11	....	7 31	....	....	7 51	....	8 118	238	418	539	119	239	419	5610	1110	2310	1041
Rectory Road	....	6 546	56	....	7 6	7 14	....	7 34	....	....	7 54	....	8 148	268	448	569	149	269	449	5910	1410	2610	1044
Stoke Newington	6 536	566	587	37	167	217	307	487	52	....	7 568	1	8 168	278	468	579	169	279	4610	1110	2710	1046
Stamford Hill	6 566	07	17	67	117	207	247	407	44	....	7 588	4	8 188	308	489	09	189	309	4810	310	1810	3110	1048
Seven Sisters	6 597	27	37	87	127	227	287	447	46	....	8 18	68	218	328	519	29	219	329	5110	610	2110	3410	1051
Seven Sisters ...dep.	....	7 5	....	7 137	247	287	447	48	....	8 8	4	8s23	8 348	54	....	9 239	349	55	....	10 2310	3510	1053
West Green	....	7 8	....	7 167	277	317	477	51	....	8s7	....	8s25	8 378	57	....	9 269	379	55	....	10 2510	3810	1056
Noel Park *	....	7 12	....	7 207	317	357	517	55	....	8s11	....	8s29	8 419	1	....	9 309	419	59	....	10 2910	4210	1059
Palace Gates †	....	7 15	....	7 237	347	387	547	58	....	8s14	....	8s32	8 449	4	....	9 339	4410	2	....	10 3210	4511	2
Bruce Grove	7 17	57	67	11	....	7 257	297	457	49	....	8 38	98	238	358	539	59	239	359	5310	3610	1053
White Hart Lane	7 47	87	97	14	....	7 287	327	487	52	....	8 68	128	268	378	569	79	269	379	5610	1110	2610	3910	1056
Silver Street ‡	7 77	117	127	17	....	7 317	357	517	55	....	8 88	158	288	408	589	109	289	409	5810	1310	2810	4211	1
Lower Edmonton 306	7 107	137	147	19	....	7 337	377	537	57	....	8 118	178	318	428	9	4 9	129	319	4210	1110	1610	3110	4411	1
Bush Hill Park	7 147	177	187	23	....	7 377	417	578	1	....	8 148	218	348	459	49	159	349	4510	1410	1910	3410	4711	4
Enfield Town ...arr.	7 167	227	217	26	....	7 407	448	08	4	....	8 168	248	368	489	69	189	369	4810	1610	2110	3610	5011	6

Down. Week Days—Continued. / Sundays.

	aft	aft	aft	aft	b	aft	aft	ngt.		mrn	mrn	mrn	mrn	mrn	aft
Liverpool Street..dep	1045	11 0	1115	1130	1145	1215	....	....		6 10	....	....	8 25	8 55	1125
Bethnal Green	....	11 4	....	1134	....	1219	....	....		6/15	....	....	8 29	8 59	1129
Cambridge Heath	....	11 6	....	1136	....	1221	....	....		6/18	....	8 31	9 1	1131
London Fields	....	11 9	....	1139	....	1224	....	....		6/20	....	8 34	9 4	1134
Hackney Downs	1053	1111	1123	1141	1153	1226	....	....		6/23	....	8 36	9 6	1136
Rectory Road	1055	1114	1126	1144	1156	1229	....	....		6/26	....	8 39	9 9	1139
Stoke Newington	1057	1116	1127	1146	1157	1231	....	....		6/28	....	8 41	9 11	1141
Stamford Hill	11 0	1118	1131	1148	12	1233	....	....		6/33	....	8 45	9 15	1145
Seven Sisters	11 2	1121	1134	1151	12 4	1236	....	....		6/38	....	8 47	9 17	1147
Seven Sisters ...dep.	1123	....	1153	....	1238	....		7 49	8 19	....	8 49	9 19	1149
West Green	1125	....	1155	....	1240	....		7 52	8 22	....	8 52	9 22	1152
Noel Park *	1129	....	1159	....	1244	....		7 56	8 29	....	8 56	9 26	1156
Palace Gates † ...arr.	12 2	....	12 2	....	1247	....		9 59	8 29	....	8 59	9 29	1159
Bruce Grove	11 5	1123	1136	1153	12 6	1208	....		6/40	....	8 50	9 20	1150
White Hart Lane	11 7	1126	1139	1156	12 9	1241	....		6/42	....	8 53	9 23	1153
Silver Street ‡	1110	1128	1142	1158	1212	1243	....		6/45	....	8 56	9 26	1156
Lower Edmonton 306	1112	1131	1144	12 1	1214	1246	....		6/51	....	9 29	3212	2
Bush Hill Park	1115	1134	1147	12 4	1217	1249	....		6/54	....	9 59	3512	5
Enfield Town ...arr.	1118	1136	1150	12 6	1220	1251	....		6 57					

* Noel Park and Wood Green. † Wood Green. ‡ Station for Upper Edmonton.

NOTES.

b Through Train to Palace Gates.

E or **e** Except Saturdays.

h Stops to set down.

S or **s** Saturdays only.

☞ **For other Trains**

	BETWEEN	PAGE
	Liverpool Street and Hackney Downs	312
	Liverpool Street and Lower Edmonton	304
	Seven Sisters and Palace Gates	311

BECKTON and STRATFORD.—Great Eastern.

Miles	Up.	Week Days.						Sundays.	
		mrn	mrn	aft	aft	aft	aft	mrn	mrn
	Beckton ...dep	6 20	1128	2 31	....	4 185	271015		6 27
2	Vic. ⎰ (Custom Hse.).	6 27	1135	2 38		4 245	331021		6 33
2¼	Docks ⎱ (Tidal Basin)	6 29	1137	2 40		4 265	361024		6 36
3	Canning Town	6 33	1140	2 43		4 295	391027		6 39
4½	Stratford Market ¶	6 38	1147	2 48		4 335	431032		6 43
5	Stratford ** ...arr.	6 39	1148	2 49		....	1033		

☞ **For other Trains**

	BETWEEN	PAGE
	Stratford and Victoria Docks	311, 320

5

On 12 July 1920 the GER introduced what was heralded as 'The Last Word in Steam Operated Suburban Train Services'. In a leaflet issued to the public by Sir Henry Thornton, General Manager of the GER, he said "from Mondays to Fridays inclusive, during the down 'crush' period, viz. between about 5.0pm and 7.30pm, 50 per cent more trains (with proportionate additional seating accommodation) than have ever hitherto been provided in the services under notice, are scheduled to run. The figure for the up morning crush period, i.e. from about 8.0am to 10.0am, is 75 per cent; that for the Chingford line, between 7.0am and 8.0am, being 53 per cent". This gave a 50-75% increase in train frequency through a number of small but important improvements. The total cost of the scheme was £80,000: this should be compared with the estimated cost of £3 million just to have electrified the Enfield line. In excess of 200,000 people a day were using Liverpool Street at this time, with over 70,000 in each of the peaks. To readily indicate which carriages were for which class, brightly coloured strips were placed above the windows, yellow for First class, blue for Second class. It was referred to by an evening newspaper as 'The Jazz Service' and this title quickly caught on with the regular travellers. This service required trains to arrive and depart from each of platforms 1 to 4 every ten minutes, including watering, shunting, uncoupling and coupling locomotives. The schedules were very tight and the L77s and K85s proved to masters of the task. As they were introduced into service they took over from the fleet of older Holden designs. As a standard principle all engines worked bunker first to Liverpool Street, it was found that they pulled slightly better when facing the Bethnal Green bank chimney first, it was easier to maintain the boiler water level over the inner firebox crown sheet, and water cranes and coal stages were positioned to suit this running configuration.

In 1921 the Railways Act became law, (also known as the Grouping), the first paragraph of this sums up the aim: 'with a view to the reorganisation and more efficient and economical working of the railway system of Great Britain railways shall be formed into groups in accordance with the provisions of this Act, and the principal railway companies in each group shall be amalgamated, and other companies absorbed in manner provided by this Act'. This came into effect in January 1923: the GER became part of the London & North Eastern Railway (LNER). In March 1923 the LNER sanctioned Stratford Works to build a further ten locomotives, the K89 class. These were numbered 990E to 999E - the suffix 'E' indicating that they were part of the Eastern Section of the LNER. By the end of 1923 they had been renumbered prior to completion as 7990-7999, with the earlier examples being renumbered to 8000-8011. This new batch of locomotives were all fitted with 18 element Robinson superheaters (subsequent batches were all superheated); the weight of the locomotives was thus increased to 62¼ tons. These locomotives were fitted with both vacuum and air brakes which gave greater availability allowing them to be used on trains other than those fitted with Westinghouse brakes. Again in accordance with GER practice they were built as right hand drive locomotives.

The GER had adopted the Westinghouse braking system as its standard for passenger vehicles. The Stratford Works built locomotives were fitted with Westinghouse pumps and air braked from new. The first two had their pumps mounted on the front of the right tank, whilst the others had them located on the side of the smokebox. For many years the distinctive rhythmical beat of these pumps operating was a familiar sound at Liverpool Street, especially on the West Side.

7999 was to prove to be the last locomotive to be built at Stratford Works and is the sole surviving N7. An early change under the new ownership was that the LNER introduced a new classification system for all locomotives based upon their wheel arrangements - for example, the 4-6-2 Pacifics were classified with the prefix 'A', 4-6-0s as 'B' and so on. The 0-6-2 locomotives were given the prefix 'N', with the former L77, K85, and K89 classes all becoming the N7 class.

The LNER conducted a review of the many different types of locomotive they had inherited from their constituent companies. The N7 class proved to be very well suited to their suburban work and was accepted as a "group standard" locomotive. The LNER Chief Mechanical Engineer, H.N. Gresley, ordered more of the class to be built. Following Government pressure these were built at Gorton Works (in Manchester) and at the LNER Doncaster Works for three main reasons: to help the relieve the unemployment situation in the north of England, this being the early years of the Depression; lower wage rates than at Stratford; and less transportation costs for the materials. 1924 saw fifty more locomotives ordered to be built at Gorton. The first ten were finished in the latter part of 1925 and allocated at first to the King's Cross district. Gorton got the order for the next twenty, but due to the amount of work they had on the order for the last twenty went out to tender, with Robert Stephenson & Co. winning the tender. The locomotives from Robert Stephenson & Co. were delivered between October 1925 and January 1926, with five going to King's Cross, four to Neasden and eleven to Stratford. The second twenty locos from Gorton were delivered between January 1926 and February 1927: four went to King's Cross, with the remaining ones to Stratford. These were all classified as N7/1 sub-class, with reduced height boiler mountings so that they could be used on services to Moorgate over the Metropolitan Widened Lines. A significant difference was that whilst the GER built locos were built for right hand drive, the LNER ones were built with left hand drive in accordance with the LNER standard practice. The Stratford built locomotives retained right hand drive: the preserved N7 is therefore right hand drive.

The British Empire Exhibition at Wembley was opened by King George V on 23 April 1924 in order to stimulate trade and strengthen the bond between the various states. The British Empire comprised 58 territories at that time: 56 of them participated. Special trains were run from Marylebone to convey some of the 27 million people who visited the exhibition: six N7s were allocated to Neasden depot from May 1925 for these trains, including No. 7999. These locos were also used on some stopping trains from Marylebone to Aylesbury and Woodford Halse (near Daventry) where the Great Central had a major depot at the railway junction there.

However, they were not well received by the crews on these workings, and in due course they returned to the Great Eastern. Towards the end of 1925 four members of the class were sent to Neasden to be used on the then new LNER & Metropolitan Joint Line to Watford, which opened on 2 November 1925. Initially the service was provided with electric Metropolitan trains to Baker Street and steam hauled LNER services to Marylebone, but this was found to be excessive provision and the steam hauled services were soon withdrawn.

The programme for 1926-7 included a further sixty two N7s, ten to be built at Gorton, thirty two at Doncaster and twenty by the contractor William Beardmore & Co. of Dalmuir, Clydebank. The LNER made a number of changes to the design of the N7 locomotives. Long travel valve gear and pony trucks were fitted to the last 72 N7s, the earlier locomotives had radial trucks, and the front axles were of conventional design with no side traverse. The 32 built at Doncaster had round-top fireboxes instead of the original Belpaire design. The round-top boilers were in-line with contemporary LNER practice, they too were fitted with 18-element Robinson superheaters. The locomotives built by Beardmore were steam braked and were fitted with only vacuum train brake equipment. The Gorton built locomotives were delivered between November 1927 and February 1928, Beardmore's between July and September 1927. The Gorton engines were initially allocated to Hatfield: between 1933 and 1940, twelve of the Beardmore built engines were fitted with Westinghouse brakes and transferred to Stratford. The Doncaster locos were delivered between November 1927 and December 1928. No further N7s were built after this date, with the class totalling one hundred and thirty four locomotives. Between 1928 and 1931 the saturated steam boilers were replaced with new superheated boilers. As time progressed and modifications were made a number of sub-classes were to appear when locomotives were reclassified. As and when the N7s required new boilers all but two were changed to round top boilers. Other changes were made too such as fitting modern Ross pop safety valves in place of the older Ramsbottom type, and some N7s had Gorton chimneys fitted in place of the original GER design. From 1933 the GER built engines had their original wooden cab roofs replaced with steel ones as they went through overhaul: the LNER ones had these from new.

In the 1930s, Stratford had an allocation of 114 of the class with some of them being at the sub-sheds of Enfield Town, Palace Gates, Wood Street, Hertford East, Ilford, Brentwood, and Chelmsford.

At the very start of World War Two the N7s were heavily involved in the evacuation of children from London getting as far as Diss, Beccles, Wroxham and Downham Market. Locomotives and stock were provided by slashing the off peak train service. During the Second World War the East End of London was heavily bombed with both the docks and the railways key targets for the German Luftwaffe. Possibly somewhat surprisingly given the amount of loss of life and the damage caused the N7s did not suffer any serious damage throughout this time. A drawing survives from this time showing where new cupboards were fitted in the locomotive cabs for the crews gas masks.

(Above) Doncaster built Class N7/3 2601 at Stratford in ex-works condition in 1933 (A.N.B. Harris, courtesy of the Stephenson Locomotive Society)
(Below) Stratford built 7992 on Stratford shed in the late 1920s
(Lens of Sutton Association)

In 1943 after Edward Thompson was appointed Chief Mechanical Engineer of the LNER a start was made it trying to sort out the rather haphazard LNER numbering scheme with different locomotives of the same class in different numerical groups: this stopped because of wartime problems and other more pressing matters requiring attention. However, this was restarted in 1946 with the result that for the first time all the N7 class, regardless of variant, were grouped together as 9600-9733.

The various design changes made to the locomotives when built and during their working lives were many, unfortunately there is insufficient room here to list and discuss them all. For more in depth detail, it is suggested to consult the RCTS 'Locomotives of the LNER Part 9A'. Apart from one locomotive the N7s retained their condensing gear until the period between May 1936 and January 1938 when the gear was progressively removed: in the case of 7999, this happened in May 1937. All except the final batch of 32 Doncaster built locomotives had Belpaire boilers when new. As the Belpaire boilers became life expired they were changed at overhauls to round top boilers from 1932 onwards, although during the war reconditioned fireboxes were generally used. In the case of No. 7999, it received its round topped firebox in February 1946, and was reclassified as an N7/4, the boiler fitted when preserved dates from 1950. Only two locos were to keep their Belpaire fireboxes until they were withdrawn.

After the end of the Second World War work resumed on the extension of the Central Line of London Underground to Epping and Hainault and the electrification of the Liverpool Street to Shenfield suburban services. London Underground trains first reached Leyton on 5 May 1947, and in stages until Epping was reached in 1948. The last section from Epping to Ongar was to retain steam operation until 1957. The electric service from Liverpool Street to Shenfield started in November 1949, thus two routes over which N7s were the normal motive power went over to electric traction. Due to partially to this, and partially to the introduction of Thompson's L1 2-6-4Ts from 1945 onwards, some N7s moved away from London to more rural lines in East Anglia, working on the Harwich, Clacton, and Walton branches. Four also went to Ipswich to supplement other locomotives on the Felixstowe branch for a few years. Three went to Cambridge in 1957, and their work included some trains over the Bury St Edmunds to Long Melford line.

On the first of January 1948 Britain's railways were nationalised with British Railways being created under the overall management of the British Transport Commission. The former GER system now became part of the Eastern Region of British Railways. All former LNER engines had their numbers amended by adding 60,000 to them, the N7s therefore becoming 69600-69733. Number 999E which had become 7999, and then been renumbered to 9621 in 1947, now became 69621. To reflect the change of 'ownership', the N7s were gradually repainted into British Railways passenger livery, black with red and grey lining, akin to the old LNWR passenger livery. Some of the first repainted examples were lettered 'British

Railways' in cream on the tank sides, but from 1949 this was changed to the lion and wheel symbol. This symbol was slightly modified from 1954, and gradually many N7s received the modified version. From early days under the new British Railways ownership seven N7s were allocated to Colwick to work suburban services in the Nottingham area, and later on four went to Neville Hill for suburban services around Leeds.

From June 1949, eleven locomotives were converted for working push-pull trains. At first only locos built by Beardmore were involved, with the locomotive steam braked and vacuum ejectors for the train brakes. These conversions were put to work on a variety of routes including a short lived shuttle service between Marylebone and South Ruislip, on the London Transport line to Chesham, between Finsbury Park and Alexandra Palace, the Romford to Upminster and Grays line, and on Midland & Great Northern Railway services around Yarmouth. Two of these were also fitted with tablet exchanging equipment. However, their main sphere of operations continued to be in the London area, and included some boat trains from Liverpool Street to the Royal Albert Docks in connection with P&O and some other liners. Two N7s (69633 and 69634) had a special modification for working the Buntingford branch of a stop valve on the boiler, needed to supply steam at Buntingford to provide steam for a water lifter used to fill the depot water tank from a well.

N7/5 69633 arriving at Mardock in 1956 with a train for Buntingford with Driver Arthur Sullivan in charge. (D Lawrence, Photos Of The Fifties)

*(Top) 69719 calls at Hackney Downs with an Up working, 29 September 1960
(Lower) 69621 leaves Canning Town with the 7.10pm (SX) North Woolwich to
Stratford Low Level on 15 June 1962 (both G.D. King)*

(Top) 69647 at Hoe Street Walthamstow circa 1958
(Lower) N7 69731 departing from Walton-on-the-Naze with the 2.48pm to
Liverpool Street on 17 June 1957. This would be attached at Thorpe le Soken to a
portion from Clacton with a fresh locomotive working to London Liverpool Street
(both Rail On Line)

Between 1951 and 1956 some N7s were fitted with silencers for the Westinghouse pump exhausts because of complaints about the noise from people living in the vicinity of Chingford station. This seems somewhat strange considering the N7s had been in service for thirty years by this time!

In 1956 one of the GER built locos No. 69614 (originally 992E) achieved celebrity status when it became the West Side pilot loco at Liverpool Street, with fully lined black livery, red coupling rods, all exterior metal fittings polished or burnished. In order to maintain its appearance, the firemen were given an additional half an hour's pay every shift for polishing it. It was withdrawn in December 1960.

In 1958 N7 69617 was immaculately turned out to haul the Royal Train between Kings Lynn and Wolferton. The first N7 to be withdrawn was 69689 in December 1958, this locomotive had retained a Belpaire boiler right to the end.

Until the beginning of the 1960s the N7s were still seen regularly at Liverpool Street, as well as on the North Woolwich to Palace Gates trains, and the branch between St Margarets and Buntingford. Electric services from Liverpool Street to Chingford, Enfield Town, Hertford East, and Bishops Stortford began on 21 November 1960, which really marked the beginning of the end for the N7s. Almost immediately withdrawn was No. 69611 - originally GER No. 1011, the last locomotive built under GER management. After this the remaining locos were used on various minor workings such as North Woolwich to Palace Gates passenger trains and Chingford branch freight until 9 September 1962 when all steam workings to the south of March were finally withdrawn and the last eight N7s were withdrawn, including 69621.

With particular reference to 69621, it started a peripatetic lifestyle from late 1948 onwards, seeing a series of allocations as follows:

November 1948	allocated to Parkeston
September 1951	allocated to Stratford
July 1952	allocated to Colwick
February 1953	allocated to Woodford Halse
June 1953	allocated to Colwick
April 1954	allocated to Stratford
May 1957	allocated to Lowestoft
September 1959	allocated to Stratford

In 1961 there was a real prospect of the former industrial line operated by the Middleton Railway Preservation Society having colliery traffic over it again. At over 100,000 tons per year this needed much bigger motive power than they had available. Dr. R. F. Youell, a lecturer at Leeds University, founder member of the Middleton Railway Preservation Society, and GER enthusiast felt that 69621 would fit the bill, capable of pulling hard and the ability to go round sharp curves found on industrial lines. So it was that after withdrawal 69621 was purchased by

69614 heads the RCTS special at Canonbury on 31 March 1959
(C. Gammell, Photos of the Fifties)
69621 departs Liverpool Street with the LCGB Great Eastern Suburban Rail Tour
on 28 April 1962 (Rail On Line)

Dr. R. F. Youell even though the locomotive latterly had a reputation as being a very poor steamer. 69621 was initially moved to Neville Hill depot in Leeds for storage. However, subsequently a change of policy by the Coal Board resulted in the closure of Middleton Colliery. With reduced space available on the Middleton Railway due to land being taken for motorway construction 69621 remained in storage at Neville Hill depot.

In 1973 BR advised that the space at Neville Hill was needed. With no action from the Middleton Railway the locomotive was offered a home back in former Great Eastern Railway territory at Chappel & Wakes Colne, base of the Stour Valley Railway Preservation Society now the East Anglian Railway Museum. An epic journey south by rail followed, departing Neville Hill towed by a diesel locomotive at 04:52 on 3 September 1973. Delayed en-route by a hot box, a freight train derailment, and the need to keep the loco out of the way as it was restricted to a maximum speed of 20 mph, saw the journey take almost fifty hours to reach Colchester. On 9 September 1973, it was moved on to Chappel: the yard is located alongside the Marks Tey to Sudbury branch line and at that time no longer had a direct connection. The British Rail branch line track had to be slewed across overnight by SVRPS members to make a temporary connection to the track in the yard at Chappel: once 69621 had been shunted into the yard by one of the SVRPS steam locomotives the branch line track was re-instated for BR trains the following day.

On 9 September 1973 after arrival at Chappel by means of a track slew, 69621 is hauled down the yard by Gunby (G.R. Mortimer, A.T. Wallis collection)

Sadly, whilst in store at Neville Hill, several components including the water gauges, vacuum ejector, hydrostatic lubricator, safety valves, injector steam and clack valves, snifting valve covers, and the whistle and whistle valve all went missing and have never been traced. Thankfully other components specific to the N7s such as the injectors and air brake components were not touched. Finding suitable replacement parts was a long and expensive process. In 1989, as a tribute to the designer, 69621 was named A J Hill. The loco was gifted to the East Anglian Railway Museum by Dr Youell on 4th April 1996.

For over forty years the N7s were a part of the railway life in East and North East London, and 69621 is a fitting memorial to the class.

69621 in store at Leeds Neville Hill in April 1964 (Rail On Line)

The original restoration

Prior to the overhaul starting the loco was repainted for static exhibition in GER passenger livery, it remained so for a few years until work could start. Number 1001 was the only 0-6-2T to ever carry this livery in service, our loco built by the LNER in 1924 never carried that livery as far as is known. Most of the initial overhaul work was carried out in the open just to the south of the Goods Shed, the workshop facilities at this time were located in the Goods Shed. When the Restoration Shed was built and made available towards late 1985 the loco was moved inside it and the overhaul completed under cover. All of the workshop facilities had to be moved out of the Goods Shed into the Restoration Shed, this work diverted much labour away from the N7 while it took place.

The cab, tanks, bunker, and boiler were all removed before the frames were jacked up for the wheels to be removed as were the connecting and coupling rods, valve gear, crossheads, slide bars, valves, and pistons. The tyres on all wheels were found to be not too badly worn although in need of attention.

The wheels were sent away for the tyres to be re-profiled and axle journals to be machined. The axleboxes were sent with the wheels to be re-white metalled and machined. Initially they went to Derby Works: Derby found they could not fit the four feet ten inch diameter driving and coupled wheels on their wheel lathe so the wheels and axleboxes were sent to Swindon Works.

Meanwhile the hornblocks were checked for alignment and trued up as necessary. The N7 has adjustable wedge axleboxes so the fixed front face had to trued up to the frames and cylinder block, then the wedges and rear faces had to be trued up to the corresponding front face. All of the axlebox springs were inspected for worn or broken leaves and buckles, (the buckle goes around the centre of the spring leaves and holds them tightly together), the six driving and coupled axle springs were re-conditioned. The front axlebox side control springs were also inspected and passed as fit for further use, the trailing truck suspension and side control springs likewise.

The big end journals on the crank axle were re-cut and cleaned up using a hand operated tool borrowed from the North Yorkshire Moors Railway. New big end brasses were cast using patterns made by a pattern maker at BT Research Laboratories during his lunch breaks. All the motion was inspected, eccentric sheaves were found to be satisfactory and the straps attended to. Most of the valve gear pins were life expired so were replaced with new ones manufactured by a member and Nitride hardened at Paxmans works. The expansion links and die blocks were inspected and refitted, new trunnion bushes in which the expansion links are mounted were fitted. The die blocks went missing for several weeks before being found: a lesson in looking after and storing parts correctly! The slidebars were re-ground prior to being refitted: the N7s have a single slidebar per cylinder design which makes re-alignment and fitting easier. It was decided to modify the crossheads, originally the white metal was applied direct to the crossheads, which is fine for the flat top plate, but the main body forging is a massive lump to heat up and remetal. Therefore brass plates were fitted both top and bottom, these were white-metalled and screwed into place top and bottom using brass screws, the screw heads being countersunk and the tops white-metalled over after fitting. The sides have dovetails cut into them to help secure the whitemetal so these were used to hold white-metalled brass side plates instead.

Quite a lot of work was found to be required on the chassis. The rear buffer beam was found to be badly bent. It was removed and taken to The Welding Institute near Cambridge for straightening out, after which it was rivetted back on, the rear buffer beam is held in place by 72 rivets!

The main air reservoir casting was removed for inspection and testing. This is a huge casting located under the cab, it also acts as a frame stretcher and contains both the main air reservoir and the locomotive air brake reservoir. The casting was in surprisingly good condition but the frames were another story, almost rusted through where over many years ash and coal had lodged in a small gap between the steel frames and the iron casting. Steel tends to suffer more badly from rust than cast iron does and the traces of sulphur in the coal and ash mixed with water created an acidic cocktail guaranteed to cause corrosion. The frames are closer together under the bunker than forward of the cab to allow greater sideways travel for the radial truck under the bunker. The point at which the frames reduce in width is at the air reservoir casting, the front bolting flanges being further apart than the rear flanges, this meant the new sections of plate had to be bent in two places prior to welding to exactly match this change in frame width. The frames were securely braced sideways and lengthways prior to the corroded sides being cut out and the new plate was welded in; it being essential that the frames remain in-line throughout and after the work. The frames and new steel plate had to be carefully pre-heated immediately prior to welding and stress relieved by more careful heating after welding. Eventually it was possible to refit the air reservoir casting in place. There were more cracks in the frames where two of the axle spring support boxes are rivetted onto the frames, these sections were also cut out and new plate welded in place.

Various other sections of platework were in need of attention. The coal bunker has a water tank located under it, this and the side tanks were badly corroded. New side tanks were constructed on site and fitted, the bunker and tank assembly was repaired as required.

Of the larger chassis mounted pipework the steel vacuum brake and air brake pipework was found to be corroded and had to be renewed, the copper steam heating and air brake pipework was reused. Most of the lubrication system was redesigned during the overhaul, two six feed mechanical lubricators were fitted, one for the six driving and coupled axleboxes instead of conventional oil boxes with trimmings, and the other for the piston valves and cylinders instead

The N7 being stripped ready for the boiler to be lifted (EARM collection)

of the missing hydrostatic lubricator. This meant very nearly all the lubrication pipework was changed.

All four of the cylinder drain cock pipes were missing and new pipes and union nuts made, the very small radius one hundred and eighty degree turns in the rear pipes were a particular challenge to achieve without the copper pipe flattening.

The cylinders, pistons, and valves were found to be in relatively good condition although required all of the ring grooves to be re-machined parallel and of course new piston and valve rings fitted. The piston rod metallic packings were completely worn out, new cast iron packings were sourced from the Severn Valley Railway and fitted. There are no packings on the valve spindles, being only subject to only exhaust steam pressure they are not necessary, theoretically the bronze valve spindle guide bushes being a snug fit prevent excessive steam leakage from around the spindles. However, when worn there is a great deal of steam leakage through them and the valve spindle guide bushes were very badly worn requiring new guide bushes to be made and fitted. The design of the valve spindles and bushes proved to be a weakness and source of trouble with the locomotives in service. The later locomotives fitted with long travel valves had a modified design of bushes with larger diameter valve spindles but despite this the valve spindles and bushes remained problematic throughout.

The steam ports and valve chests in the cylinder casting were very badly choked with carbon from excess steam oil. The the hole through the blastpipe was down to about 2" diameter instead of the much larger diameters it should be tapering in to about four inches at the blast nozzle.

The choked blastpipe nozzle would have severely hampered the free flow of exhaust steam out of the cylinders and up the blast pipe thus reducing the free running and haulage capacity of the locomotive. The reduced blast would also have significantly reduced the steaming capability of the boiler. The boiler was also found to be very badly fouled with limescale, again adversely affecting the steaming capability of the boiler. 69621 had a reputation as being weak and a poor steamer at the end of her service on BR and this would go some way to explain why.

Difficulties were experienced in removing the carbon from inside the valve chests and steam ports. After several days with hammers and chisels, and a pneumatic descaling tool the remaining carbon deposit was removed using the trick of lighting a small wood fire inside the valve chests to burn out the carbon. These thick layers of carbon were the result of repeated excessive cylinder lubrication over quite a long period of time, the carbon coming from the thick heavy grade cylinder oil.

Moving on to the boiler, the tubes, flues, superheater and header, and regulator valve were removed, about a ton of scale removed from inside it before an internal inspection could commence. All of the firebox stays were re-headed inside and outside, (working inside the inner firebox is a hideous job due to the copper oxide dust that defeats dust masks and tastes absolutely foul).

*(Top) The frames, wheels and motion, tanks and cab refitted, awaiting boiler,
23 August 1987 (Peter E Thompson)*
(Lower) Refitting the boiler into the frames in 1990 (Fred Tanton)

Several foundation ring rivets had to be replaced and all of the crown stay nuts renewed. The superheater flues were deemed to be suitable for further service so new "bottle ends" were welded onto the firebox ends and machined ready for re-fitting. The superheater flues are screwed into the inner firebox so have a section at the firebox end that is of smaller diameter and greater wall thickness, this enables the threads to be cut without unduly thinning the superheater flue. The end of the flue resembles the top of a bottle hence the name "bottle-ends". The superheater elements were also found to be re-useable so new ends were welded onto them and pressure tested. The superheater flue threaded holes in the inner firebox had to be cleaned prior to re-fitting the flues, they are seldom all the same diameter, one of our society members set about designing and making an adjustable tap and guide for cleaning out the threaded holes.

The main steam pipe and other internal boiler pipework was found to be re-usable. The blower supply pipe from the steam dome to the front tubeplate was removed, the original design of blower valve was mounted inside the smokebox and it was very badly corroded, a new blower valve was fitted on the backhead and new pipe run along the top of the right hand side tank.

Now the boiler could be re-tubed, the superheater flues installed it was made ready for the required hydraulic test. A hydraulic test involves filling the boiler completely with cold water and raising the pressure by means of a pump to the required test pressure. Then it was one and a half times working pressure plus ten pounds per square inch, so our N7 boiler was tested at two hundred and eighty pounds per square inch. Once the hydraulic tests were completed the overhauled and replacement boiler fittings were installed and the boiler made ready for an out of the frames steam test. Following successful testing the boiler was ready for re-fitting into the frames. The chassis having been re-wheeled so time previously.

The valve gear, slidebars, pistons, valves, etc., were all re-assembled prior to the boiler being put back in the frames mainly because access is much easier with the boiler out of the way. Once the boiler was back in the frames the rest of the locomotive could be refitted and the N7 started to look like a proper locomotive once again.

Numerous non-ferrous parts had gone missing between the locomotive being purchased and its arrival at Chappel as follows:-
- Safety valves, replacements obtained before the overhaul started.
 -Whistle and whistle valve, replacements provided came from a V2.
- Combination back-head clack and injector steam valves, Hunslet Austerity pattern were used as replacements but these required adaptor spool pieces to be made because the flanges on the boiler are different bolting pattern to that on the Austerity valves. The pipework was adjusted to fit.
- Hydrostatic lubricator, decision made to fit a mechanical lubricator instead, but this meant atomisers and a steam supply for them had to be fitted.

- Water gauges, BR standard pattern gauges fitted but they also needed adaptor spools because of the flange differences.
- Vacuum ejector, similar replacement ejector acquired but needed adjustments to mountings and pipework.
- Air brake drivers application valve, similar pattern item obtained.
- All pressure gauges, new items obtained.
- Most of the brass oil pots from the motion were missing, new ones were made courtesy of the Royal Air Force, and two useable second-hand ones were provided by an ex-N7 fireman.
- Much of the copper pipework was missing or in bad condition so replacement pipework was made along with making the fittings to connect it all in, also the new external blower supply and atomiser pipework. Just prior to this some suitable copper pipe was recovered from a ship at Southend, so luckily very little if any had to be bought. When the hydrostatic lubricator was removed the pipework from the cab to the cylinders was left so this pipe was reused for lubrication pipework elsewhere. Like-wise the axlebox supply pipework from the large oil boxes mounted on the back-head that originally fed the main axleboxes, these boxes now feed the trailing hornblocks, the axleboxes being fed by a second mechanical lubricator.

Finance, time, and availability determined that substitute parts were used in place of missing items rather than have exactly accurate replacements made. It was felt that mechanical lubrication should be used for cylinders, valves, and main axleboxes because it provides more reliable lubrication than the original scheme and it also supplies oil when the locomotive is shunted when cold.

The auxiliary supplies from the steam supply manifold in the cab had to be redesigned because of the atomiser steam supply required for the cylinder oil pipework, the different vacuum ejector, etc. Much of the pipework in the cab had to be redone, new valves fitted, and of course the threads in the manifold and on the pipe union nuts being re-used were the GER's own sizes, adaptors had to be made for the new valves to fit onto the manifold and for the pipe unions. Fortunately the large diameter injector and steam heating pipework was all re-useable. The original fittings such as injectors, snifting valves, steam heating valve, and so forth that we had were cleaned and serviced.

The chassis was pretty much complete and the boiler re-assembly work starting when the call came to have the locomotive to Southend for the 100th anniversary of the railway line to Southend Victoria station. This meant we were working to a deadline now and things got really hectic with people working all sorts of long hours were worked, some volunteers working seven days a week, evenings during the week and both days at weekends. For the first time contractors were employed to ensure completion by the required date. The locomotive was final steam tested then loaded onto the low-loader for transport by road to

Southend on the same day. The locomotive was still in steam, the boiler had been filled ready for steaming at Southend and the water tanks were to be drained to lower the centre of gravity during transport, the tanks were still draining down as the truck with 69621 on board departed Chappel yard for Southend!

There were numerous people involved in getting the N7 back into traffic that it is impossible to name them all. It was a remarkable effort and the appearance of 69621 at Southend and faultless running throughout the event was a tribute to all at the Museum: *the photo below shows it being loaded for the trip to Southend (G.R. Mortimer, A. T. Wallis collection)*

N7 69621 and J15 65462 in action at the North Norfolk Railway's August

008 gala, two Great Eastern Railway locomotives together (Kieran Hardy)

(above) The man who saved the N7, Dr R F (Fred) Youell, beside his loco on 15 December 1990 (Peter E Thompson)
(below) An undated view of the N7 on a passenger train at Chappel

(above) On a Driver Experience course at Chappel, 19 March 2011 (G D King)
(below) The N7 on a passenger train at Chappel, 7 August 2011 (Rob Boyce)

69621 ON TOUR

Following the completion of the restoration of 69621 in 1989, a series of visits to other heritage railways and railway open days, together with running on the national network and London Underground took place. These occurred firstly from 1989 to 1999, then from 2005 to 2015. Many of these are featured in the following pages. Since then the loco has been withdrawn for major overhaul, further details of which will follow later in this publication.

The first such outing was to the Southend Open Day held on 28 August 1989 to celebrate the centenary of the Shenfield to Southend Victoria railway line, together with the Southminster branch line. It was for a while touch and go whether 69621 would make it, but after the expenditure of much midnight oil in the previous few weeks the loco was completed and made a fine sight as it steamed within the confines of Southend Victoria yard.

69621 at Southend Victoria with 08833, the Liverpool Street pilot
(Peter E Thompson)

69621 at Southend Victoria on the shuttle service
Photo above by Peter E Thompson, photo below by Reg Batten

(Above) At Cambridge Open Day on 30 September 1989 (Mark Honeywood)
(Below) Running as LNER 7999 at the Swanage Railway Gala on
11 September 1990 (G D King)

(Above) 69621 at Bury Bolton Street on the East Lancashire Railway, 11 May 1991
(Peter E Thompson)
(Below) At Colchester Open Day, 26 August 1991 (G D King)

On 31 March 1991 the N7 visited Stratford for the closure ceremony for Stratford Major Depot (both photos Steve Allen)

(Above) N7 69621, 37350, D5583 (31165) and D200 (40122) (Steve Allen)
(Below) D4001 (08833), N7 69621, D5583 (31165) and D200 (40122) (Nick Proud)

In December 1991 and at Easter 1992 the N7 operated a series of shuttles between Marks Tey and Great Cornard. Above shows a service arriving at Chappel, below a shuttle departing Chappel (both G D King)

Above a shuttle service crosses Chappel Viaduct, below a service is seen near Jankes Green between Chappel and Bures bound for Great Cornard (both G D King)

*In 1992 the N7 visited London Underground for the Steam On The Met event,
working shuttle trains between Harrow On The Hill and Amersham
(Both Mark Honeywood)*

These photos from Steam On The Met show the N7 within the confines of London Underground depots (both Mark Honeywood)

1993 saw visits to the Severn Valley Railway (above, at Bridgnorth by Peter E Thompson) and to the Nene Valley Railway (below, at Wansford by G D King)

Above: the N7 at the EUR150 celebrations at Ipswich in 1996 (Peter E Thompson)
Below: the N7 on the Kent & East Sussex Railway in 2008 (Mark House)

The N7 visited the North Norfolk Railway on two separate occasions:
above it is at Sheringham (Rob Boyce) and below at Weybourne (Mark House)

The N7 visited the Llangollen Railway in 2008:
above is at Carrog (Mike Lake) and below at Llangollen (Mark House)

2009 saw visits to (above) Barrow Hill and (below) to the Mid Norfolk Railway
Both photos by Mark House

*(above) In 2010 the N7 received attention at Buckfastleigh on the
South Devon Railway (E W Lawrence)*
(lower)The Chinnor & Princes Risborough Railway was visited in 2011 (Rob Boyce)

(above) At the Colne Valley Railway on 26 May 2012 (G D King)
(below) A powerful departure from Cheddleton station on the
Churnet Valley Railway in 2012 (Dave Gibson)

Just before withdrawal for overhaul in 2015, the N7 is pictured running round at Leekbrook on the Churnet Valley Railway (Mark House)

The N7 on a Railway Experience course at Chappel: for further details of these popular courses please ask at the Visitor Reception or e-mail reception@earm.co.uk (Photo by G.D. King)

The current restoration

Since the N7 returned to Chappel from the Churnet Valley Railway in 2015 it was initially cosmetically restored and placed on static display pending overhaul.

In Summer 2020 a proposal was agreed to overhaul the locomotive. The decision was made that unlike the rebuild that was completed in 1991 to MT276 standard (for main line running on the national network) it would be restored for service both at the Museum and occasional visits to other railways. This was in light of the limited number of occasions it has been used on the national network and the stringent and costly requirements to attain this certification were felt not to be worthwhile.

Work started by stripping down the locomotive to establish the overall condition. A number of valve rings were found to be broken and will need replacing. The motion was examined carefully and found to be in sufficiently good condition to allow for its intended use. The boiler was found to be in need of considerable work: the front tube plate which was only replaced at the last overhaul has wastage and will need to be built up. The barrel is mostly sound but some areas of wastage will need building up. The outer firebox will require new side sheets two stays

In position prior to the boiler being lifted out of the frames (Michael Sanders)

above the expansion brackets. All the boiler work will be required to be done by specialist contractors: all other anticipated work is likely to be done at Chappel. The backhead is cracked on the radiuses and a decision has yet to be taken as to whether to repair or replace. A number of rivets will also need replacing. The copper inner firebox is basically sound and only minimal attention will be required. The wheels were turned at the South Devon Railway in 2011 and do not require any further attention. The crank axle axleboxes were also replaced at that time and are sound. The side tanks are also sound and did not require to be removed for this overhaul.

The aim is for locomotive to be completed in time for 69621's 100th birthday in 2024, but will as always depend if any additional work is found to be necessary and the availability of finance. Nobody has ever said when restoring a steam locomotive "Well, that needed less work and less money than we thought it would!".

The boiler lift in progress, the boilet being lifted on to the Lowmac wagon with the Museum's Class 04 diesel in attendance ready to shunt after the lift (Matthew Cornell)

(Above) Museum volunteers seen working on the frames after the N7 had been moved into the Restoration Shed in 2020
(Previous page top): the N7 frames after the boiler had been lifted
(Previous page lower) the Museum's Class 04 diesel locomotive seen shunting the N7 after the boiler lift
(all photographs by Michael Sanders)

DONATIONS

Donations towards the restoration of the locomotive are always very welcome, and can be made by contacting the Museum. They can also be Gift Aided to make even better use of your donation! For further information please ask at the Visitor Reception, telephone 01206 242524 or e-mail information@earm.co.uk

(Opposite top) At the North Norfolk Railway in August 2008 (Kieran Hardy)
(Opposite lower) At the Colne Valley Railway in 2012 (G D King)
(Back cover) At the closure ceremony for Stratford depot on 31 March 1991
(Steve Allen)